PREPPER PETE PREPARES

Written by Kermit Jones, Jr.
Illustrated by Christy Brill

To K, A, M, E, and L – the reasons I prepare!
– K.E.J.J.

To the people preparing to protect
and care for their loved ones in times of crisis.
– C.B.

Visit
www.PrepperPeteAndFriends.com
to learn more!

Text copyright ©2013 by Kermit E. Jones, Jr.
Illustrations copyright ©2013 by Christy Brill
Cover design & digital layout by Jeff Eskridge
All rights reserved. Published by Kamel Press, LLC
www.KamelPress.com

Library of Congress Control Number: 2013917463

978-1-62487-009-5 Paperback
978-1-62487-010-1 Hardcover
978–1–62487–012–5 eBook

Published in the USA

There once was an ant named
Prepper Pete.

When he was younger,
Pete decided he needed to be
better prepared.

Ants prep in the Spring…

Summer…

and Fall…

so they can survive the Winter.

As he grew up, Prepper Pete
discovered that there are
many different reasons to be
prepared... not just Winter!

He learned that "prepping" meant
"preparing for the future..."

...and that even the government says everyone should be prepared to live at least three days without help... just in case!

If more people are prepared, emergency workers can focus on other people with a greater need…

…like those who are in trouble or who might be hurt.

Prepper Pete learned that some people prepare
for a power outage during a storm.

He thought that was a great idea,
so he bought some candles, flashlights…

...and even a generator.

Others prepare for natural disasters,
like hurricanes, floods, or tornados.

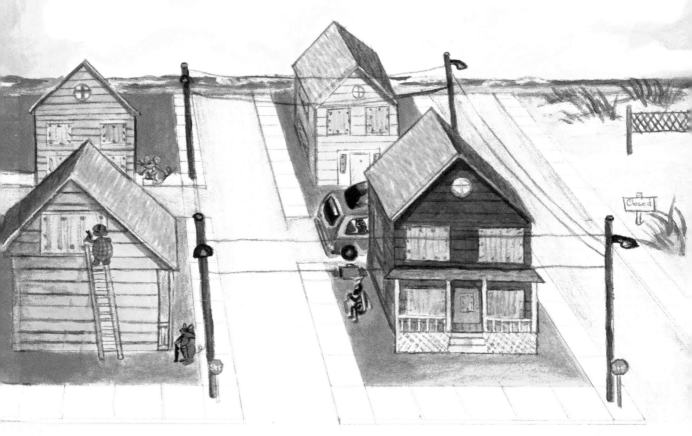

Those can mess things up really bad,
so Prepper Pete bought some tools,
extra food, and water.

He also made a safe shelter
in case his family needed it.

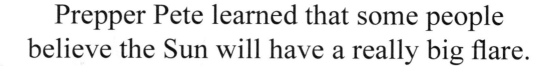

Prepper Pete learned that some people believe the Sun will have a really big flare.

Such an event could cause all electronics to stop working.

Certain types of war would also cause a similar event, so Pete started learning to use tools that didn't require electricity.

He also discovered that some people think a big sickness, called a plague, might happen.

Pete couldn't do much about that,
but he did try to live a healthy
lifestyle and exercise.

Many think the Economy might collapse, and everything will become expensive or unavailable. People might even begin to fight over food.

Prepper Pete wasn't sure, but he thought his extra food could come in handy and that being self-sufficient was a good idea.

He learned some people think
those in charge might lose control,
and the police won't be able
to protect everyone.

Others think help will
always be available, but
Prepper Pete didn't want to
take that chance.

He knew that not everyone was prepared.
Those who didn't have anything might
become desperate and try to
take things from others.

So Prepper Pete decided
to keep his prepping a secret.

Each day, Pete
tried to learn
something new.

He took a firearms safety course,
bought some guns and ammunition,
and he practiced often.

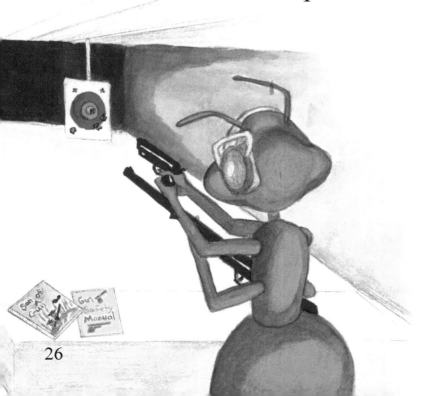

He knew these
skills could be
very useful.

He could hunt for meat...

...and protect his family from bad guys.

He began to pay off his debt,
because he didn't want to owe anyone money.

He also bought some gold and silver.

He figured these precious metals had been used as money for thousands of years, so it couldn't hurt.

He learned to plant a garden and
grow his own food.

He also bought some supplies to collect
and store water.

He was sure his family could live a
long time with little help from
others by being self-sufficient.

People who are self-sufficient
believe they should be able to
take care of themselves.

These people are called "Preppers"
because they are "preparing" for
something in the future.

Some of them, like Pete's friend,
Survivalist Sam, prefer the term
"Survivalist" because they are learning
to "survive the unknown."

If Pete and his family have to evacuate and leave their home…

…they have a plan to go and live
with their friend Sam.

Prepper Pete often tells his kids,
"Some people prepare because they are afraid."

"Our family does not have to be afraid,
because we are prepared!"

"We can sleep better at night
because we are Preppers!"

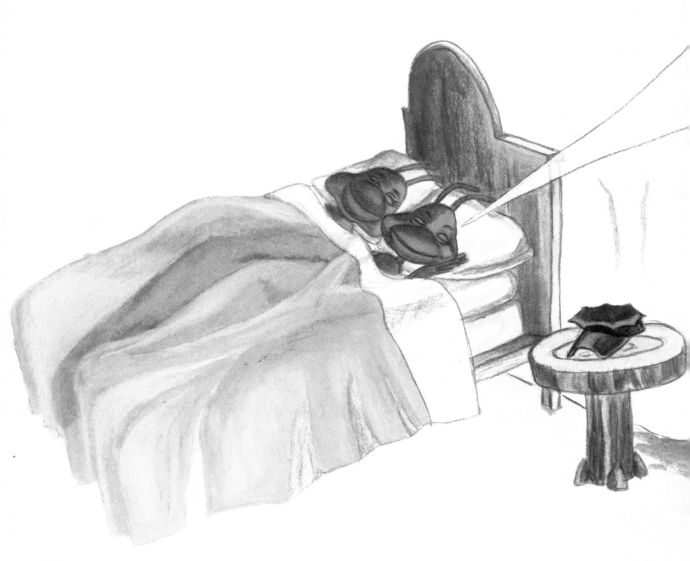

THE END.

A NOTE FOR GROWNUPS!

Teaching kids the importance of being prepared doesn't have to be harsh or scary. Regardless of why you (or someone you may know) prepare, remember that the single most important thing you can teach your kids is how to think!

All the preps in the world don't mean a thing if people don't know how to think clearly. Teach useful skills to all of the kids you know, to include critical thinking, problem solving, and the most important one of all - how to be resourceful!

KEEP PREPPIN'!

LOOK FOR THESE OTHER BOOKS ABOUT PREPPER PETE & FRIENDS!

PREPPER PETE'S TWELVE DAYS OF PREPPER CHRISTMAS

Twelve perfect gifts for the Prepper in your life! Based on a true story.

PREPPER PETE'S GUN OF A SON

When he turns old enough, Pete decides to take his son to a gun safety course where they learn important safety rules to follow.

SURVIVALIST SAM STOCKS UP

Learn about the importance of Beans, Bullets, Bandages, and Bad Guys with Prepper Pete's best friend.

PREPPER PETE GETS OUT OF DODGE

When the time comes to leave town, our hero grabs his family and takes them to safety using OPSEC (Operational Security) along the way.

Visit
www.PrepperPeteAndFriends.com
for more!

ABOUT THE AUTHOR

Kermit Jones, Jr. stumbled across the idea of a prepper book for kids when trying to decide how to explain the topic to his four young daughters. He grew up in a rural setting, and later joined the Navy, which allowed him to travel the world. Between kids and his career, he has learned that it is important to "be prepared!"

ABOUT THE ILLUSTRATOR

Christy Alexander Brill is a native of Wilmington, NC. Proudly married to a United States Marine, and the mother of three young children, she understands the importance of being prepared.